Psychedelic Dream Coloring Book

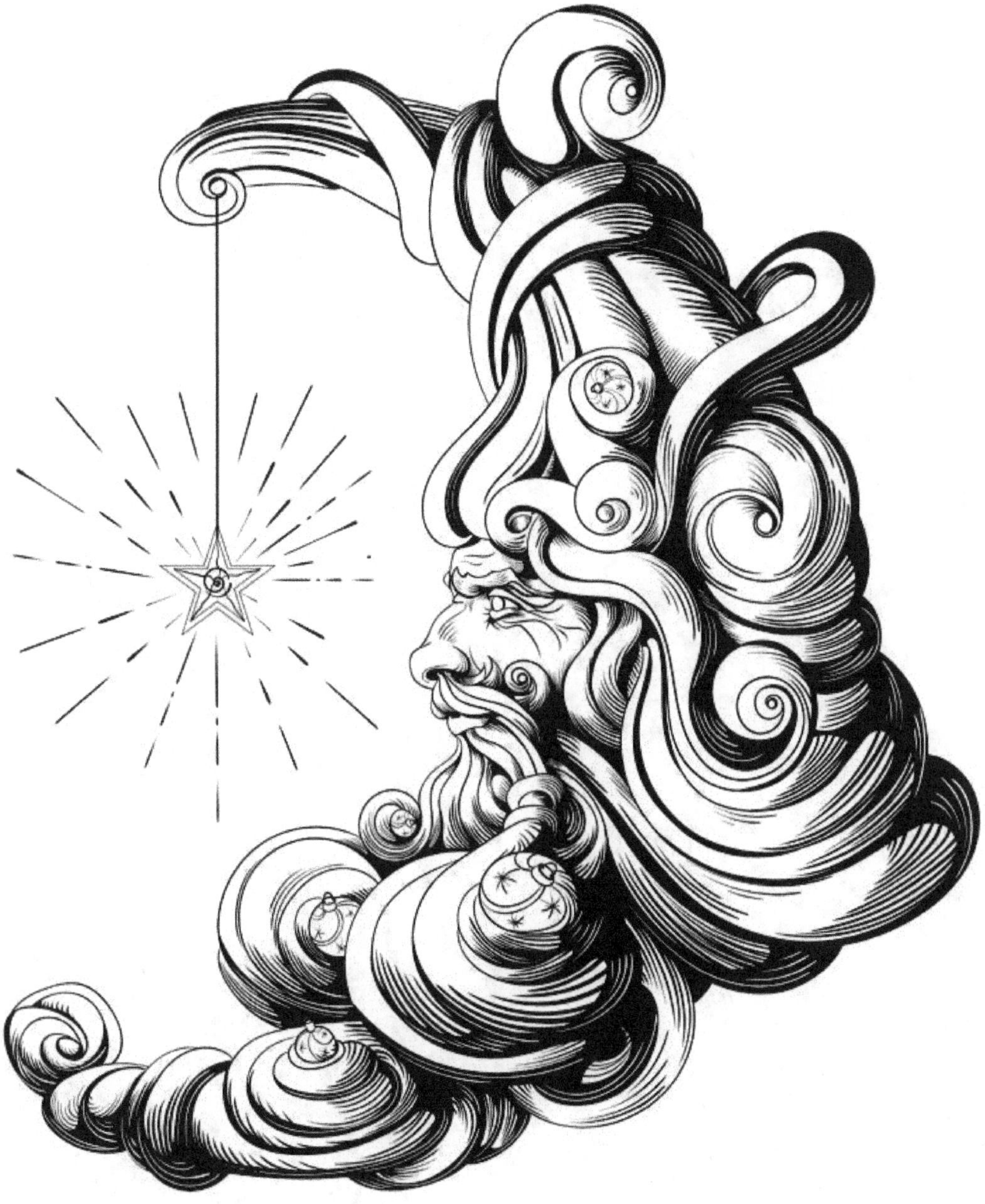

Copyright © 2020 Katrin Stark
ALL RIGHTS RESERVED

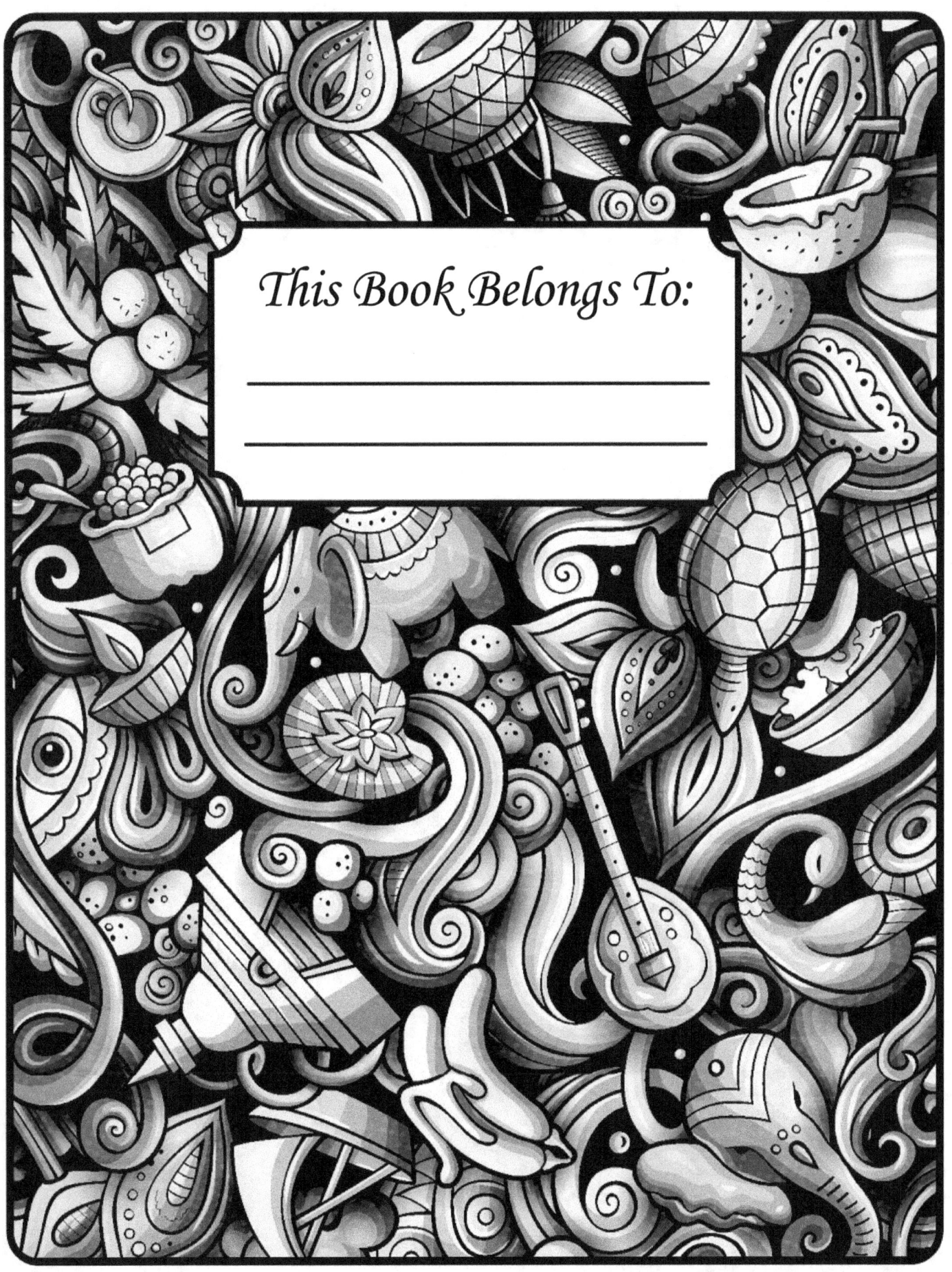

COLOR TEST PAGE

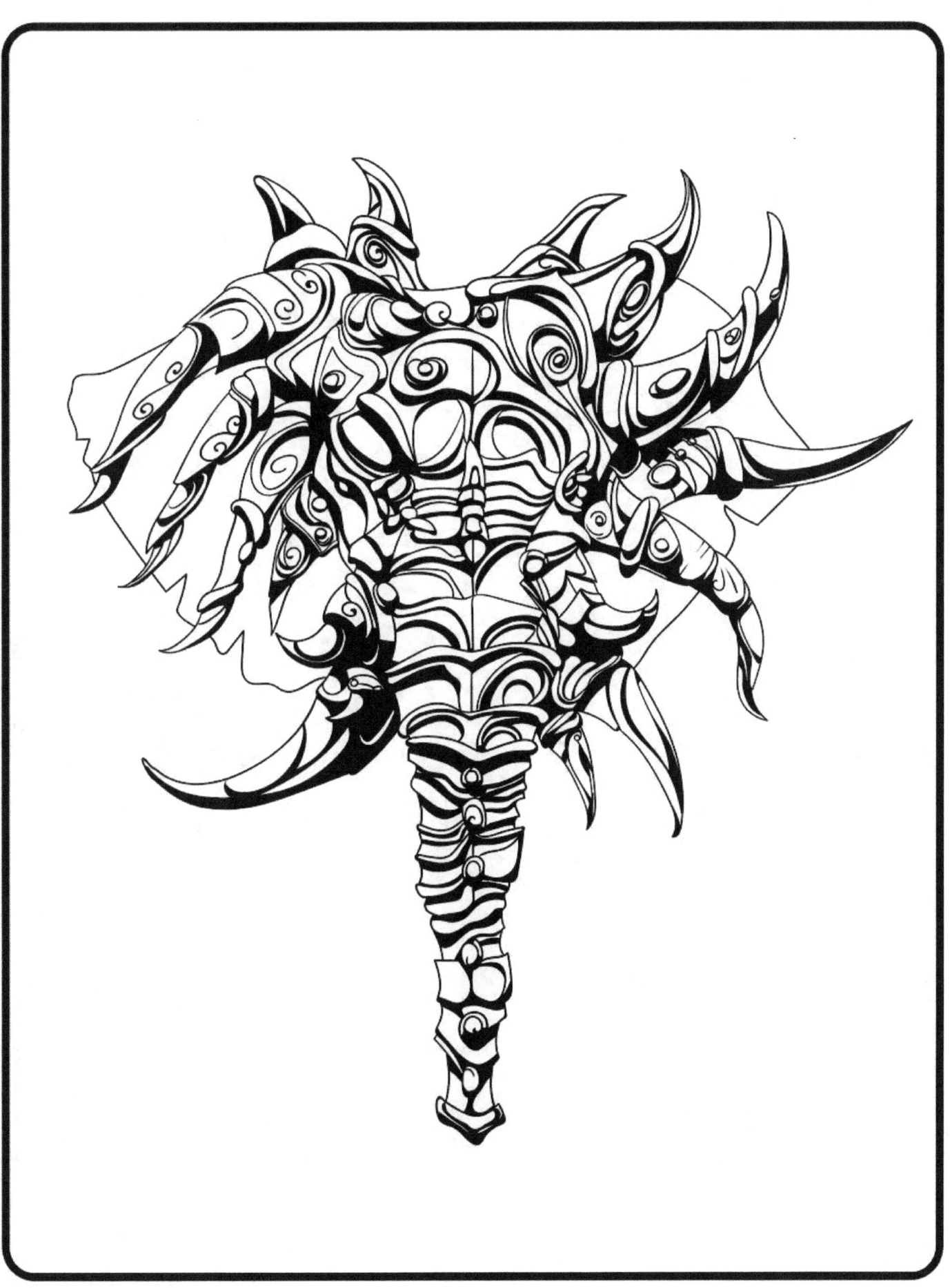

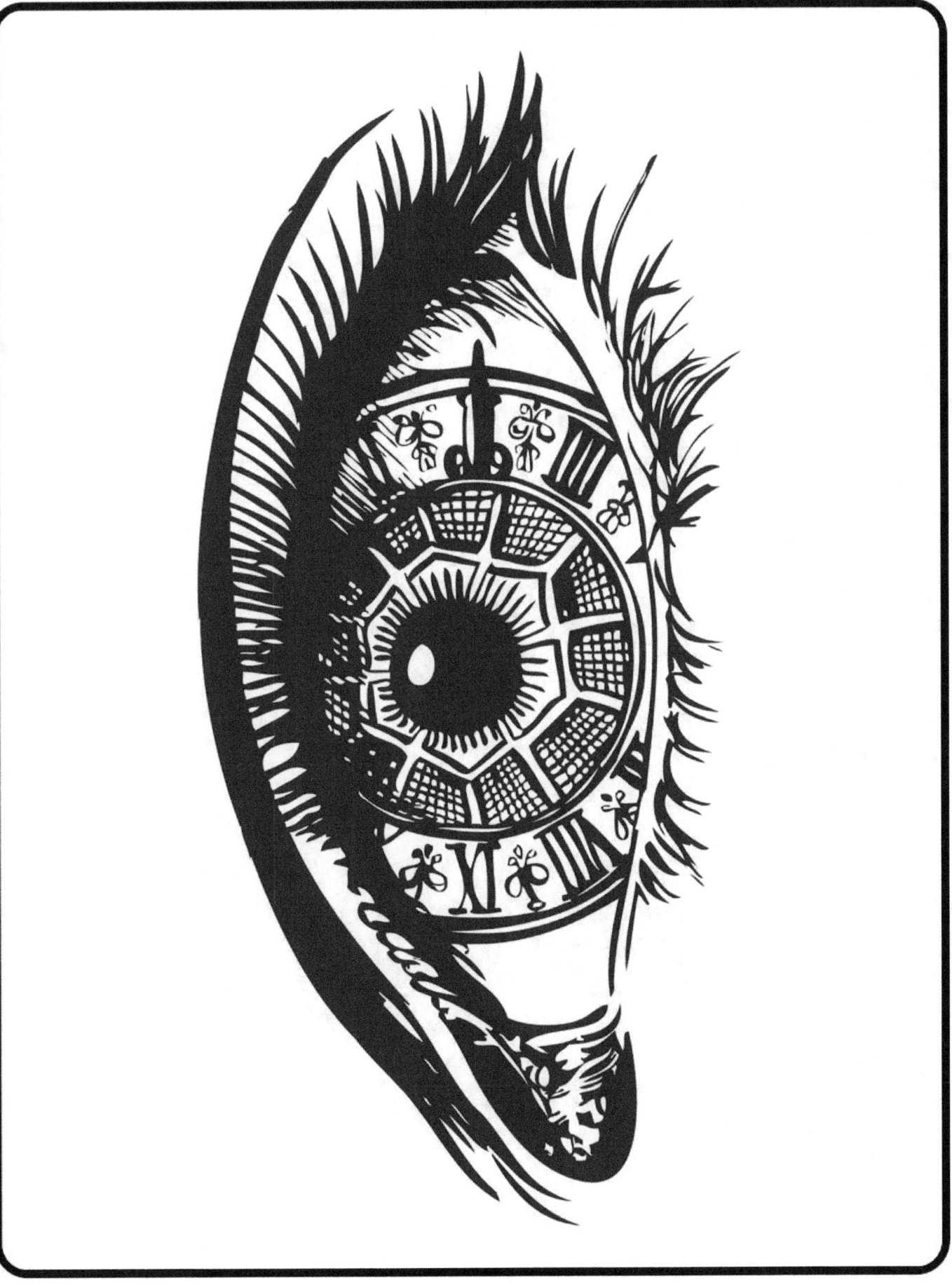

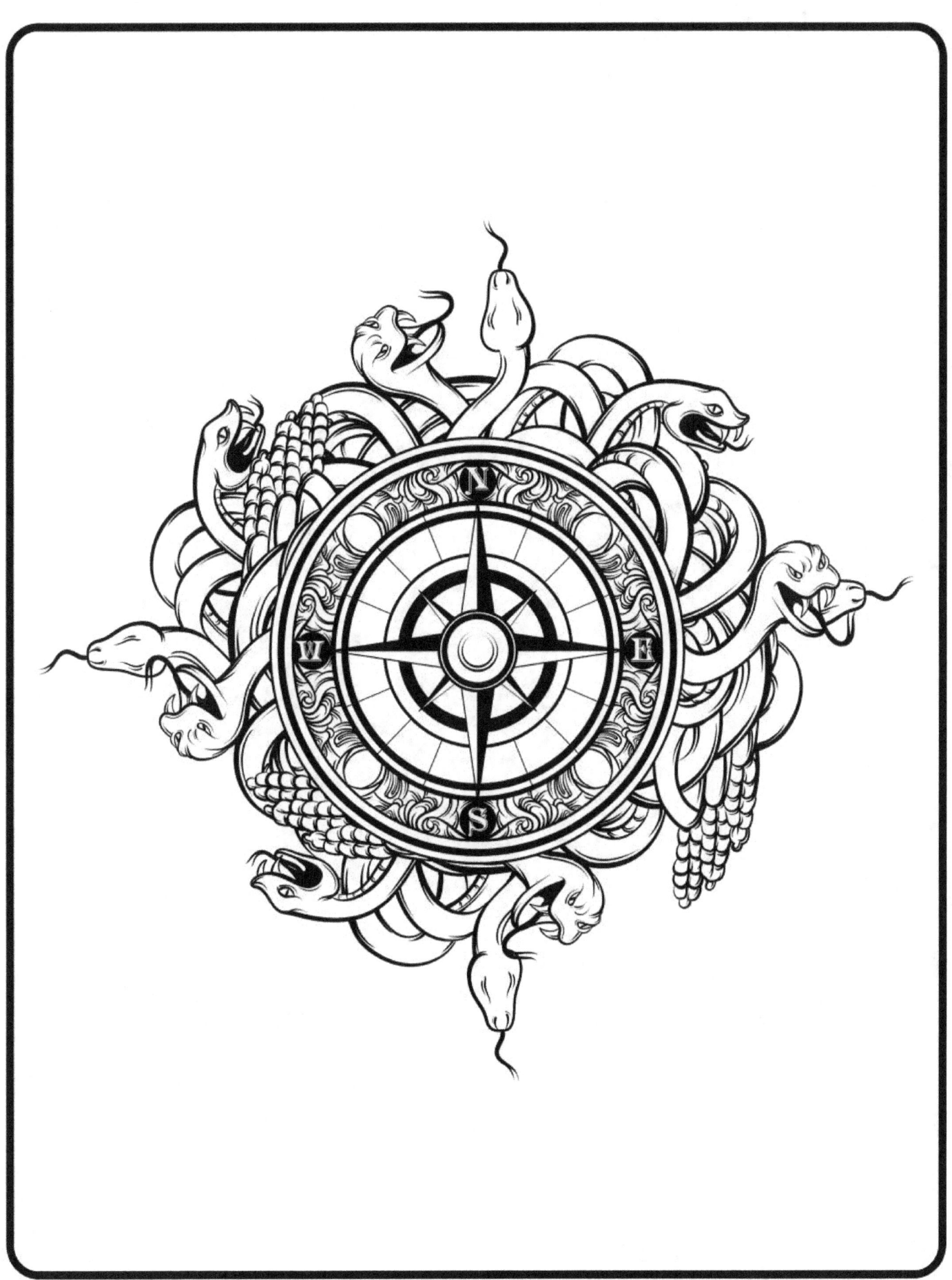

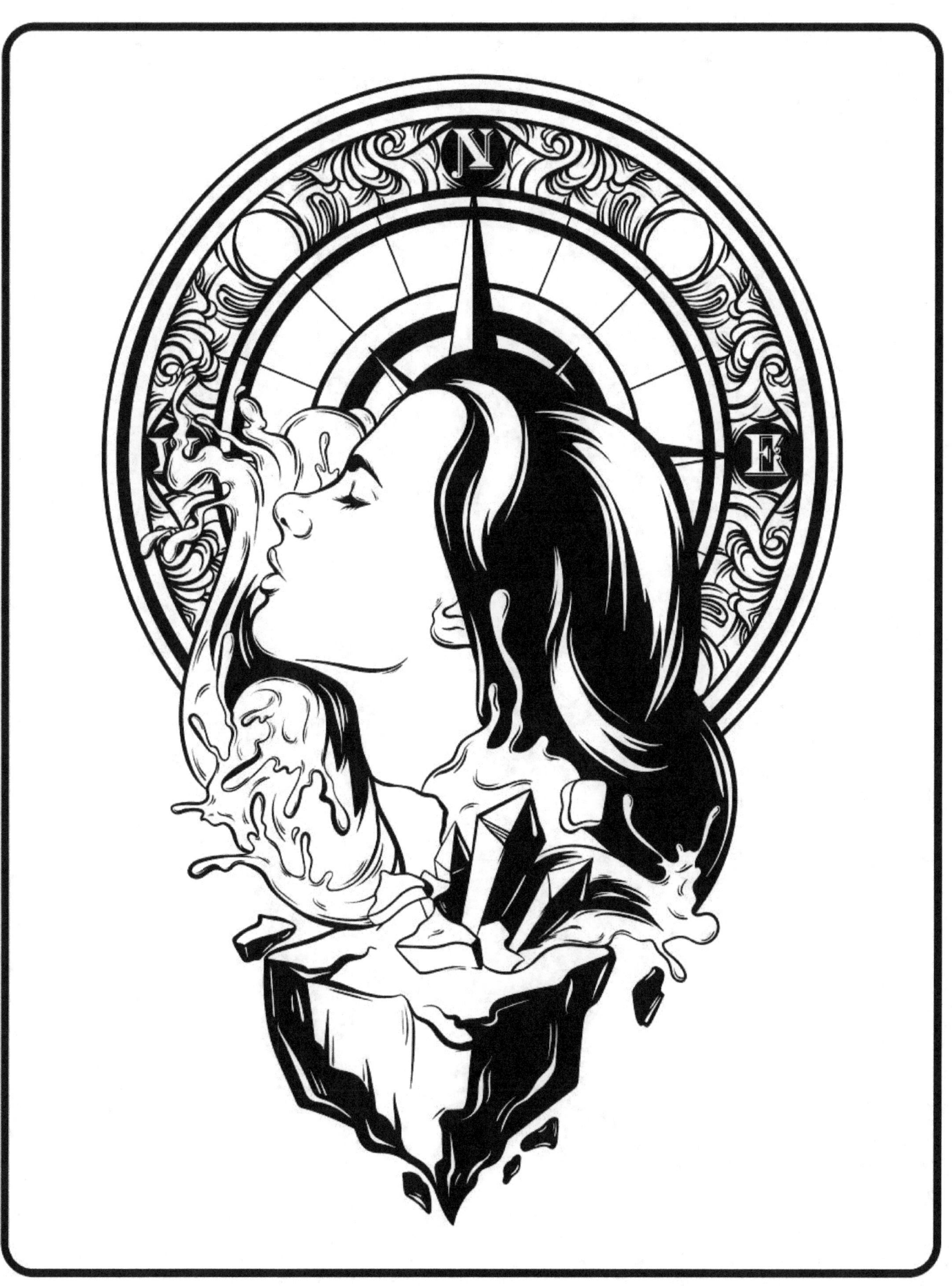

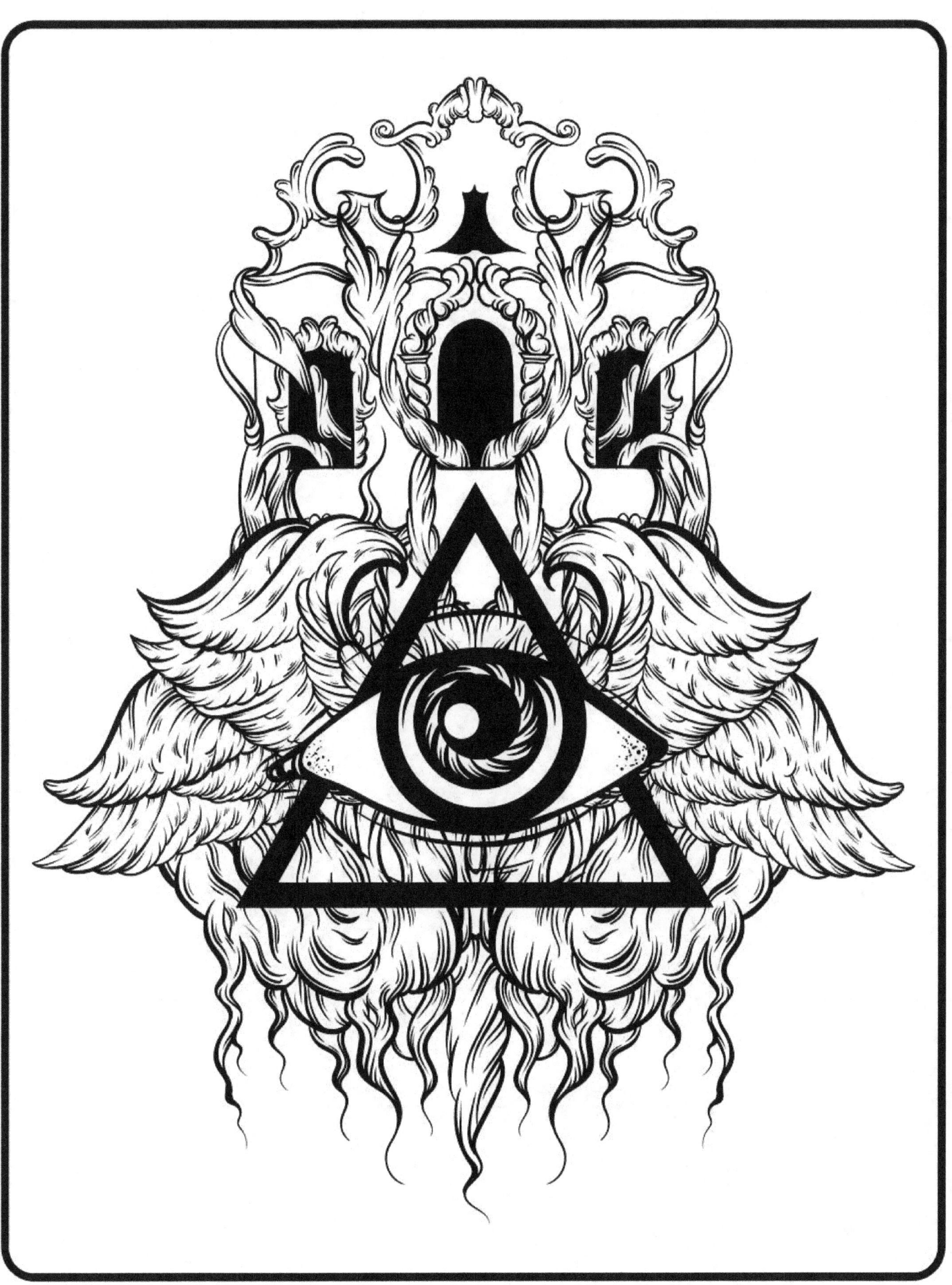

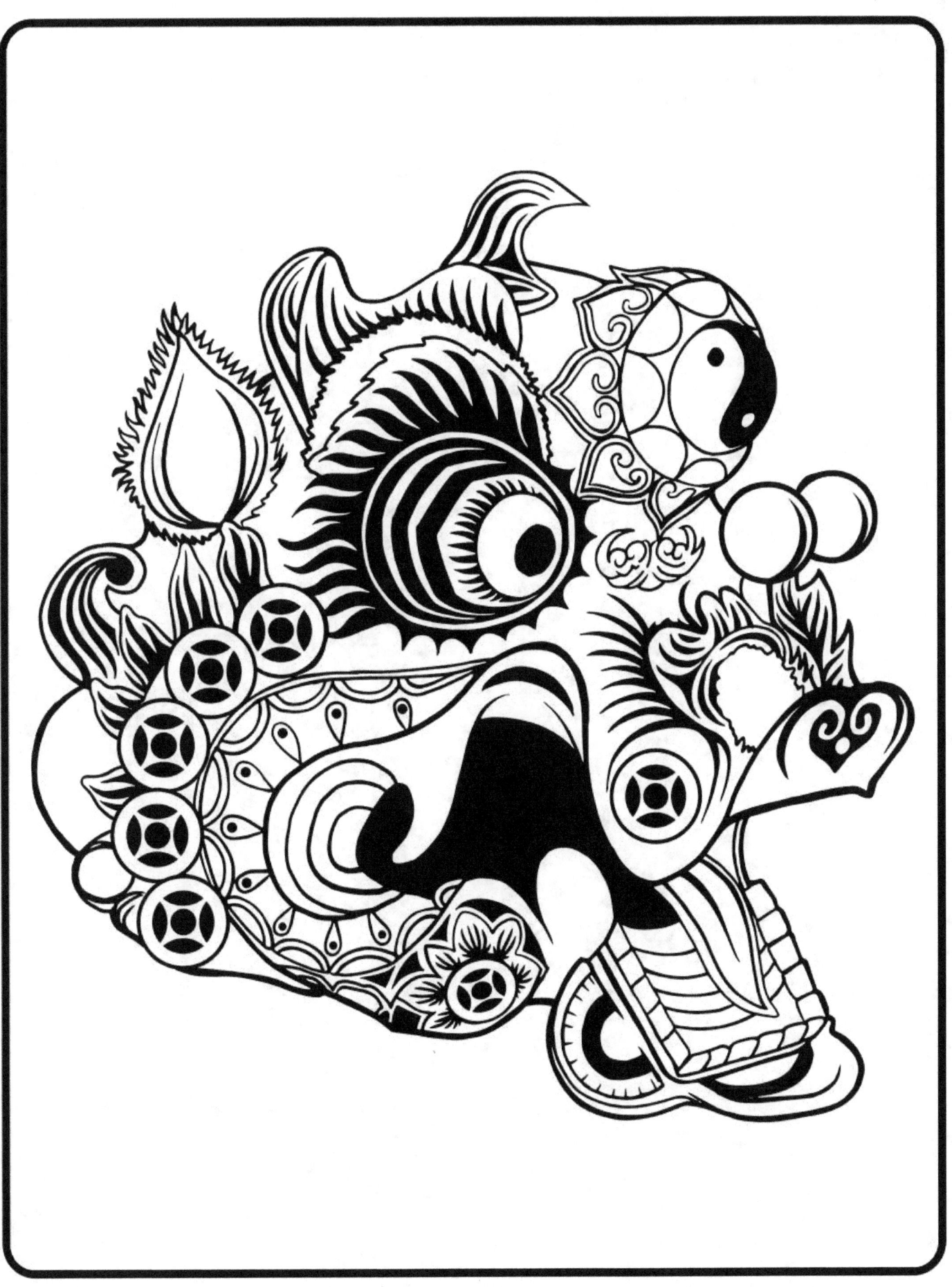

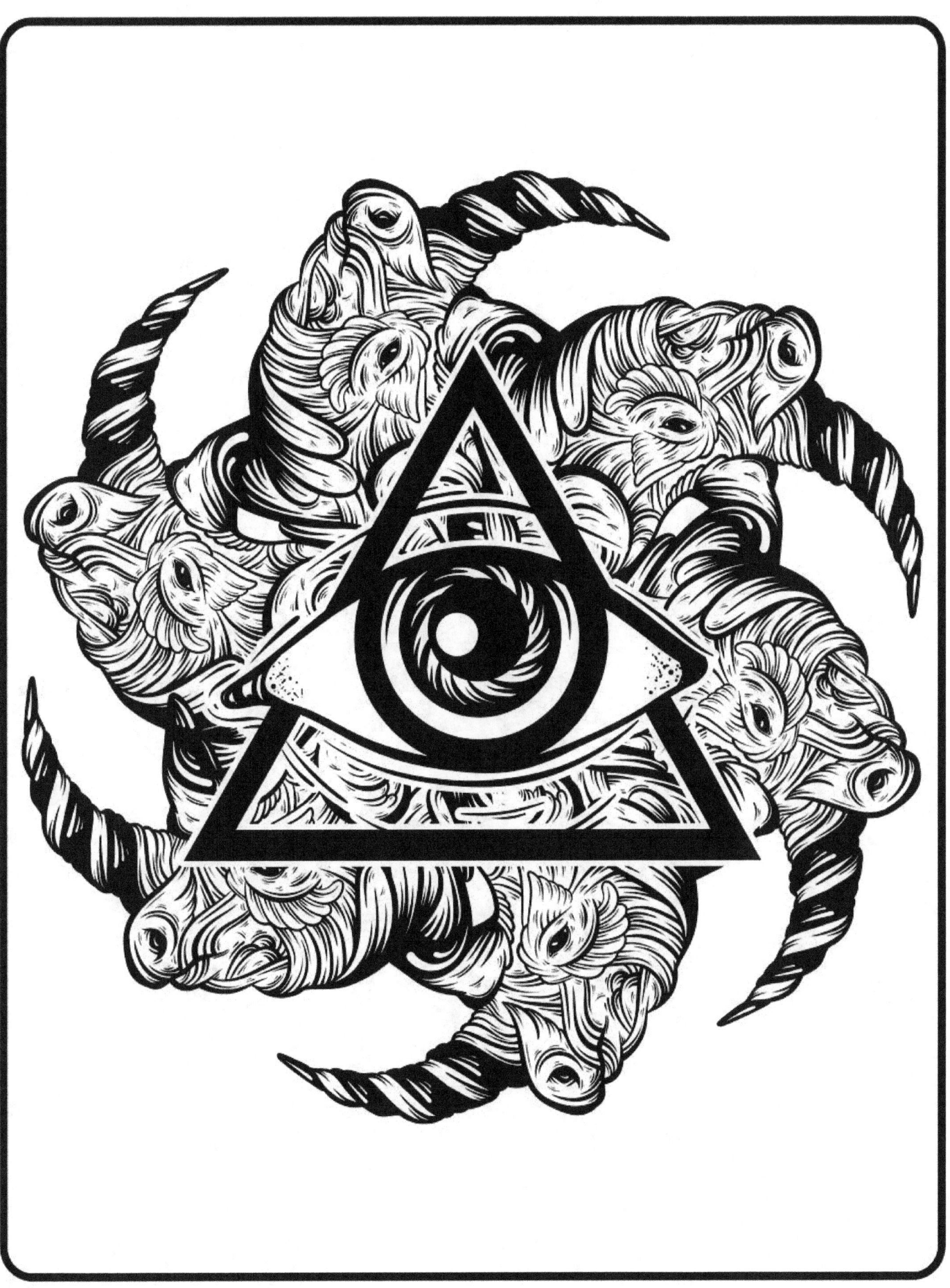

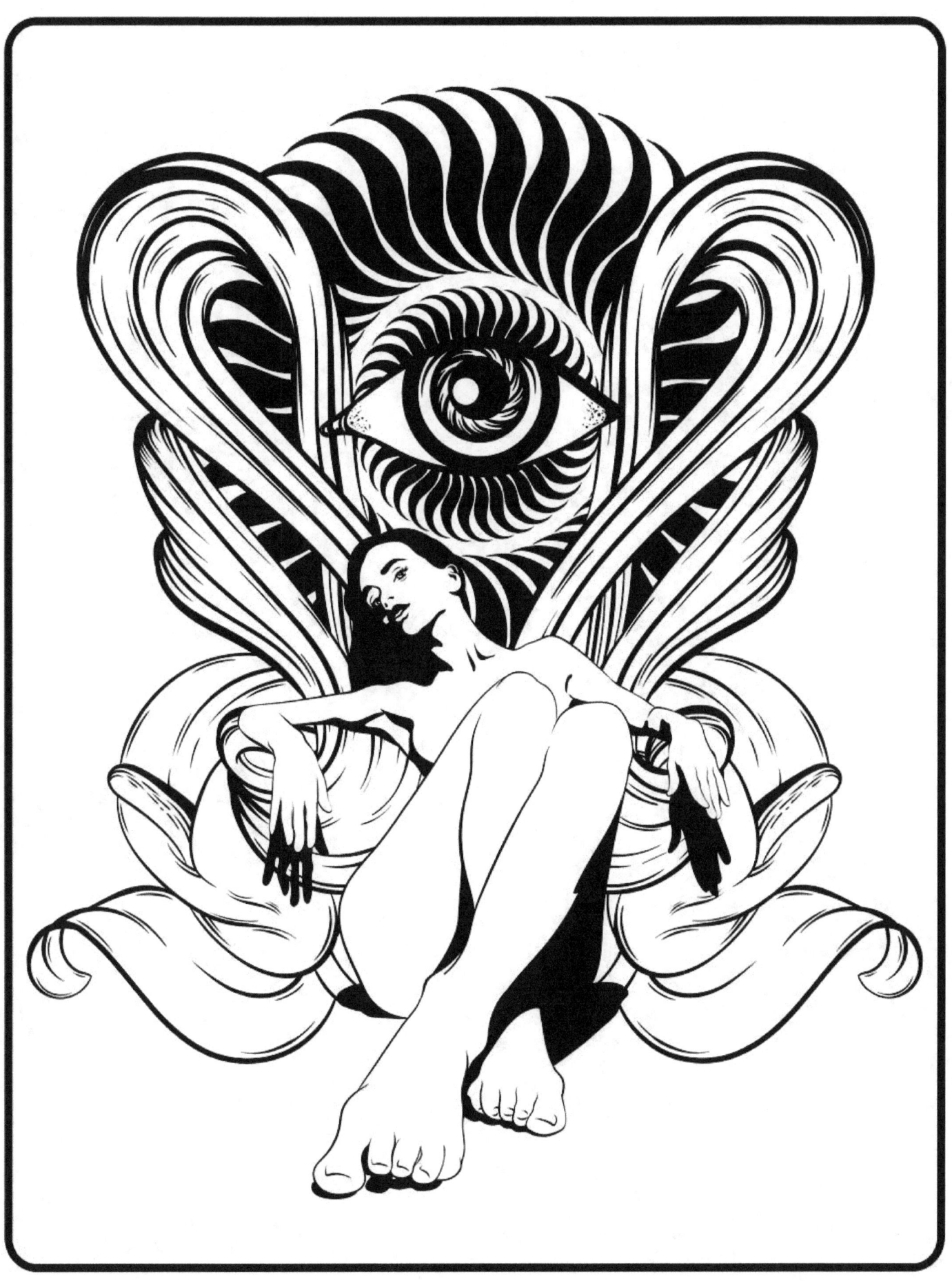

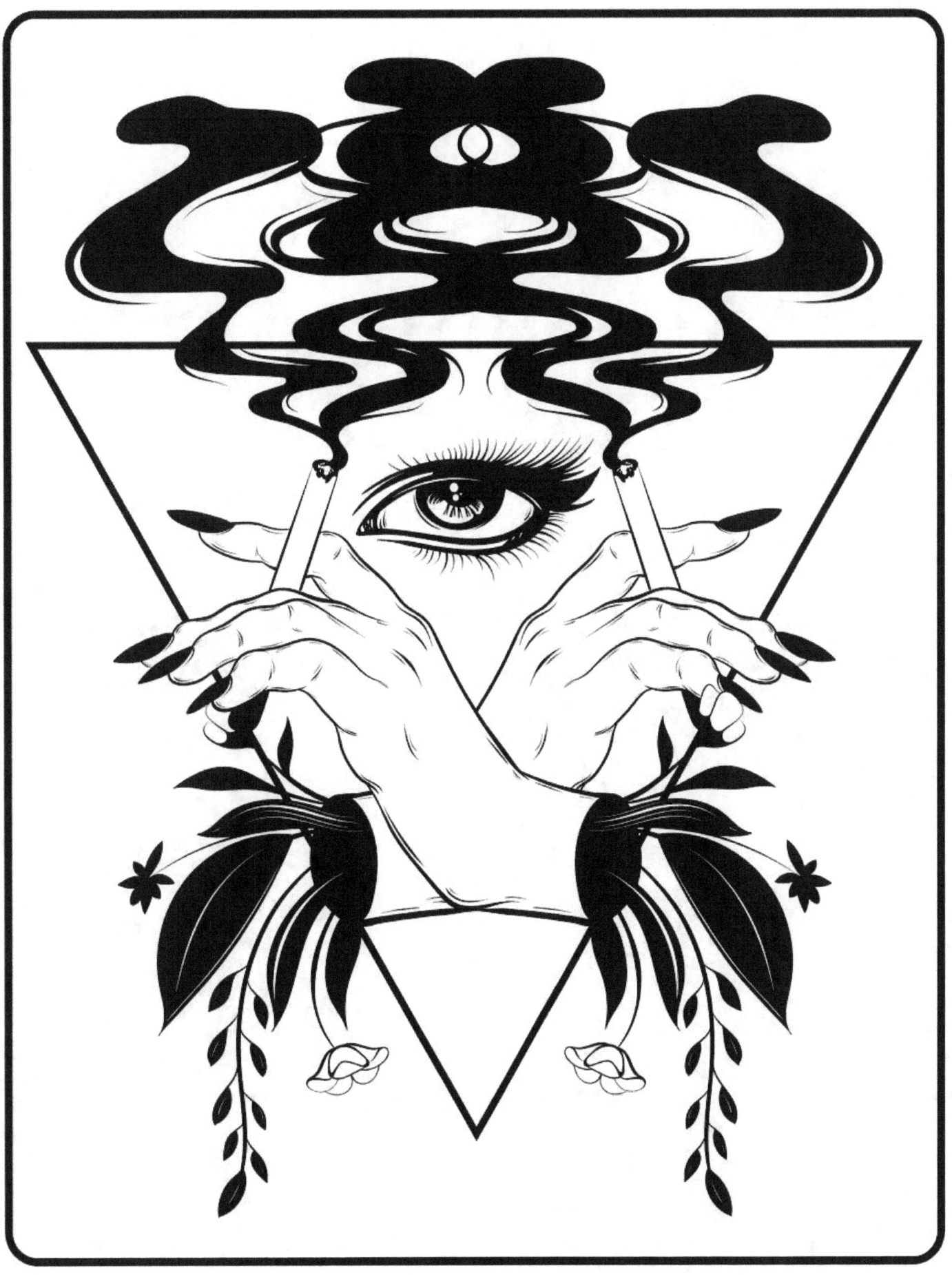

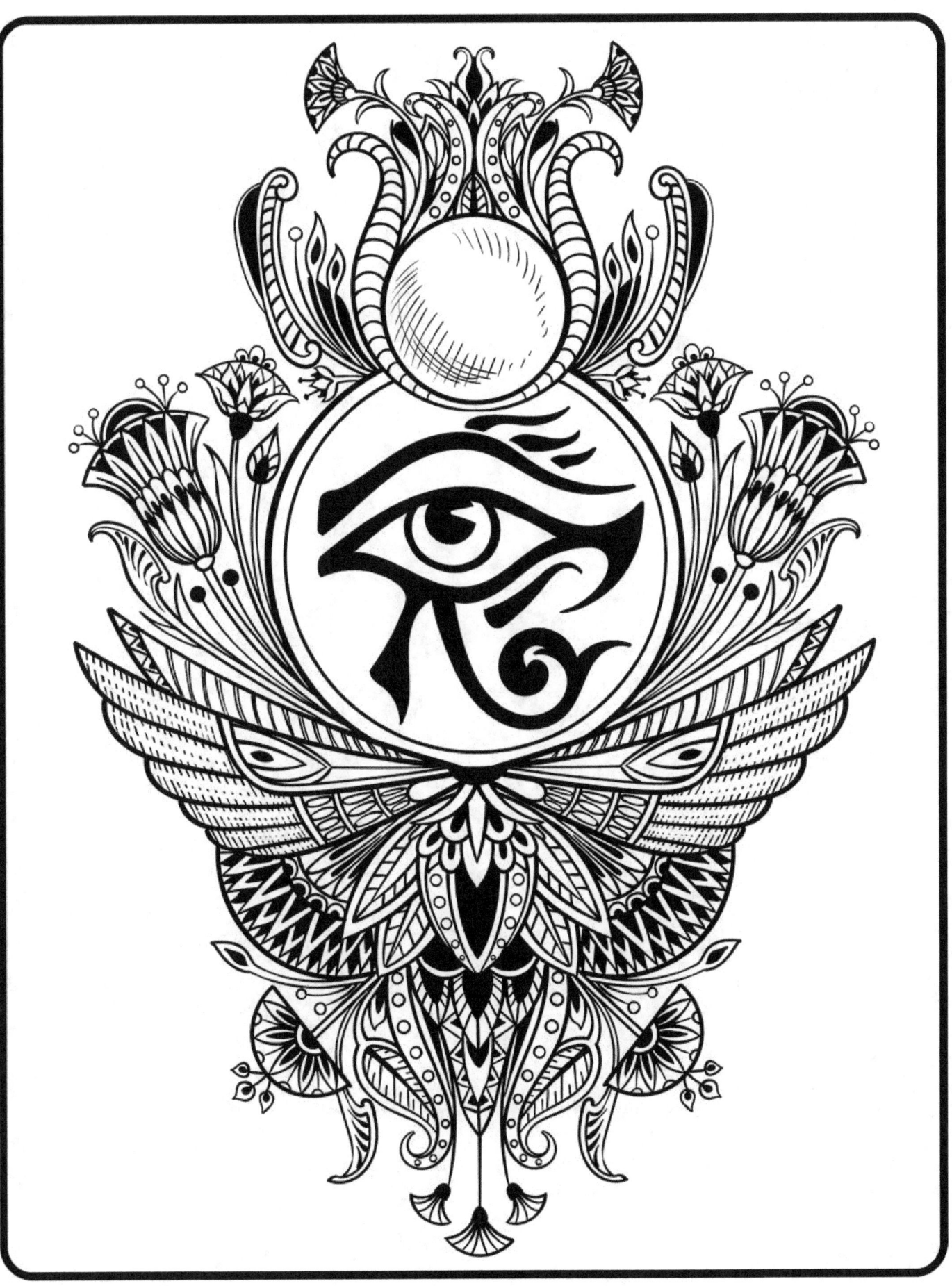

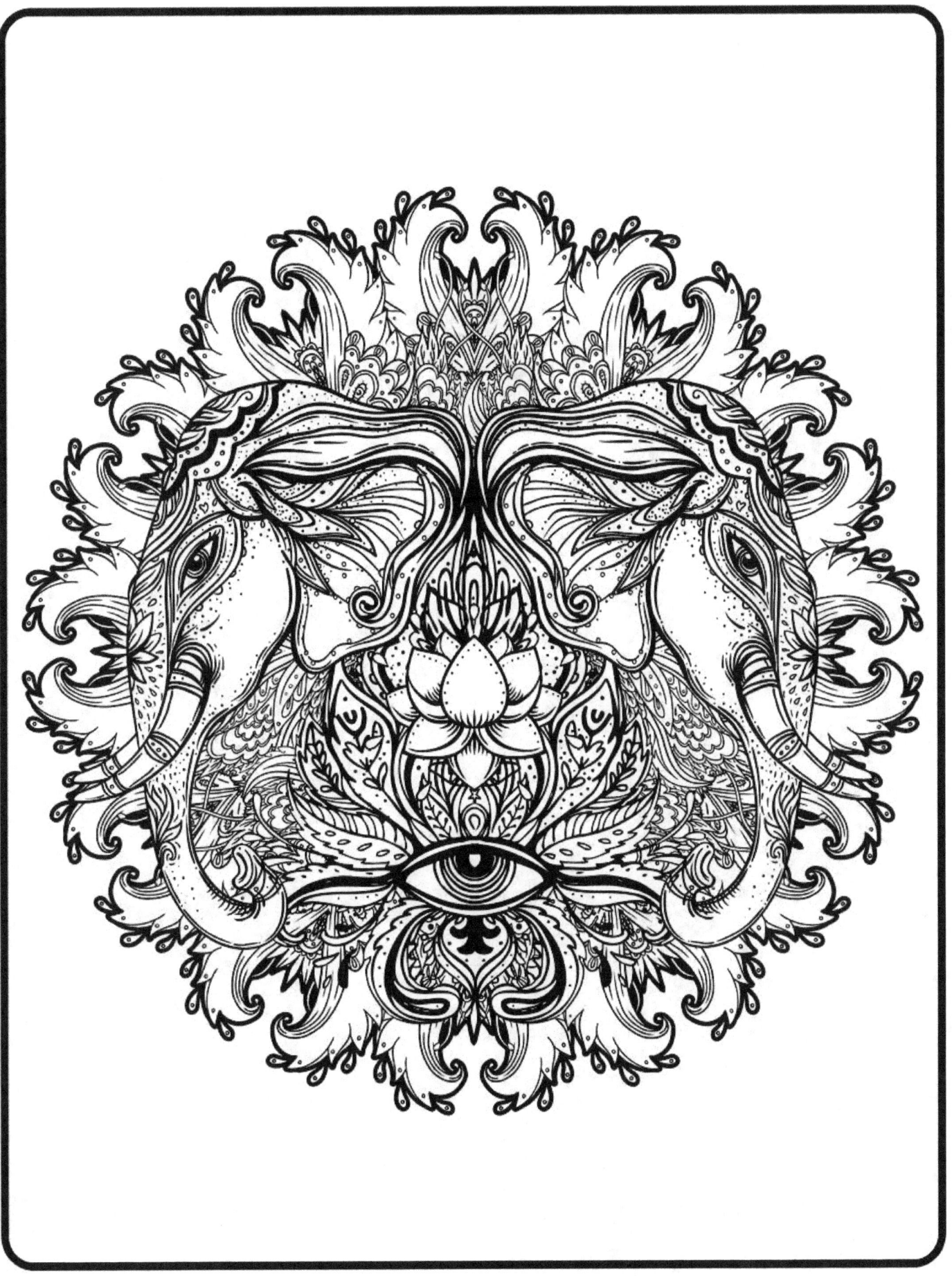

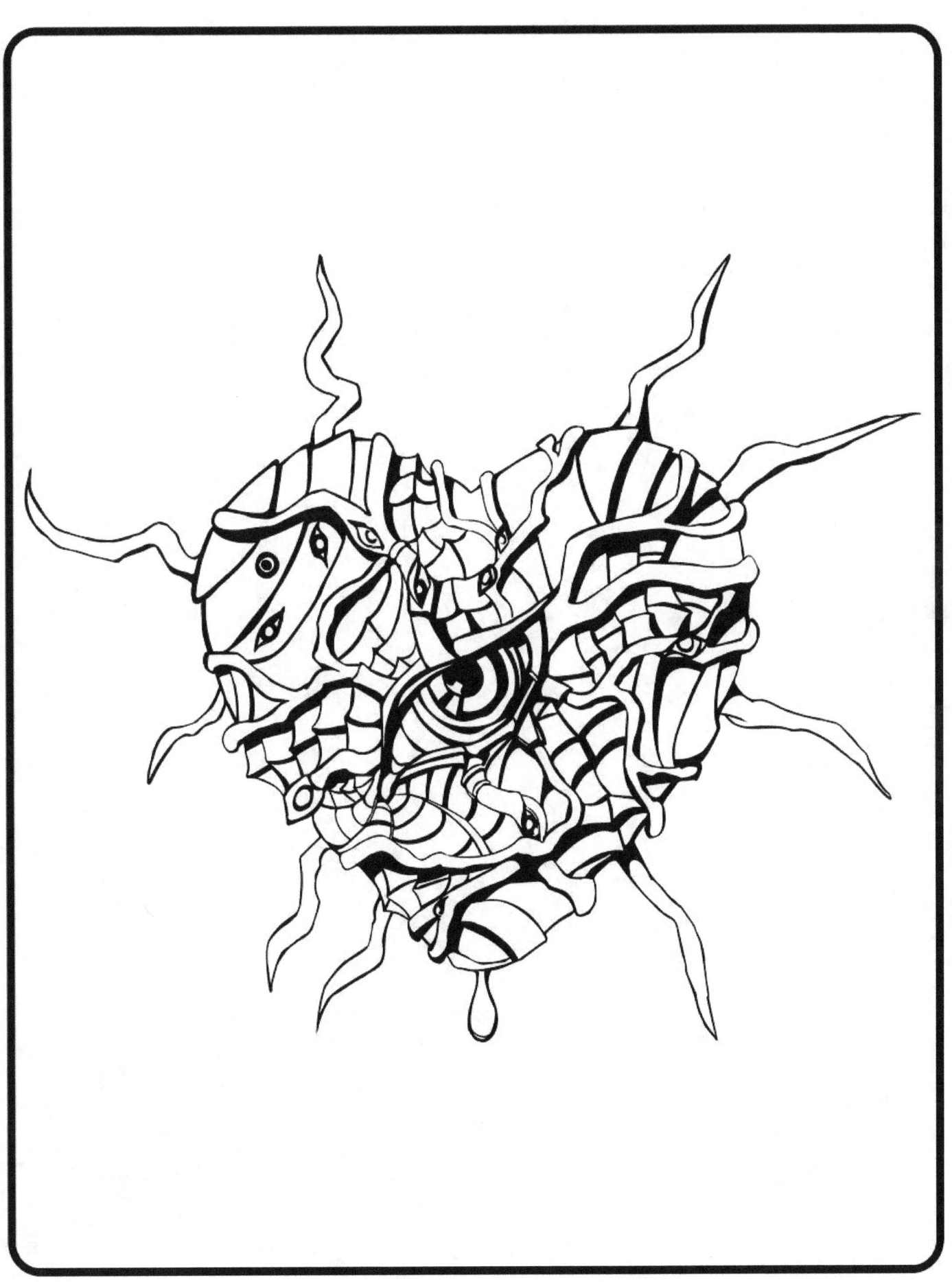

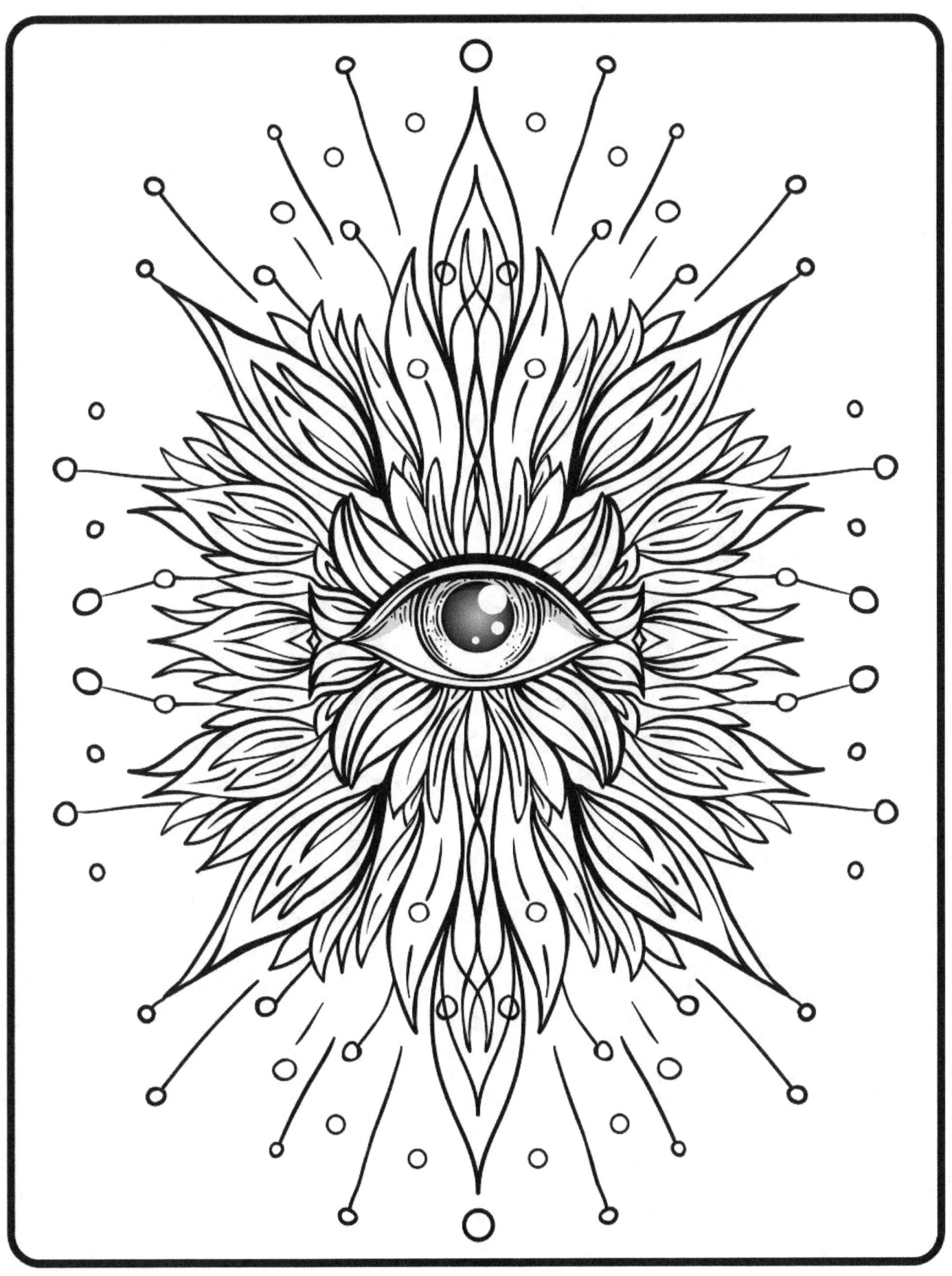

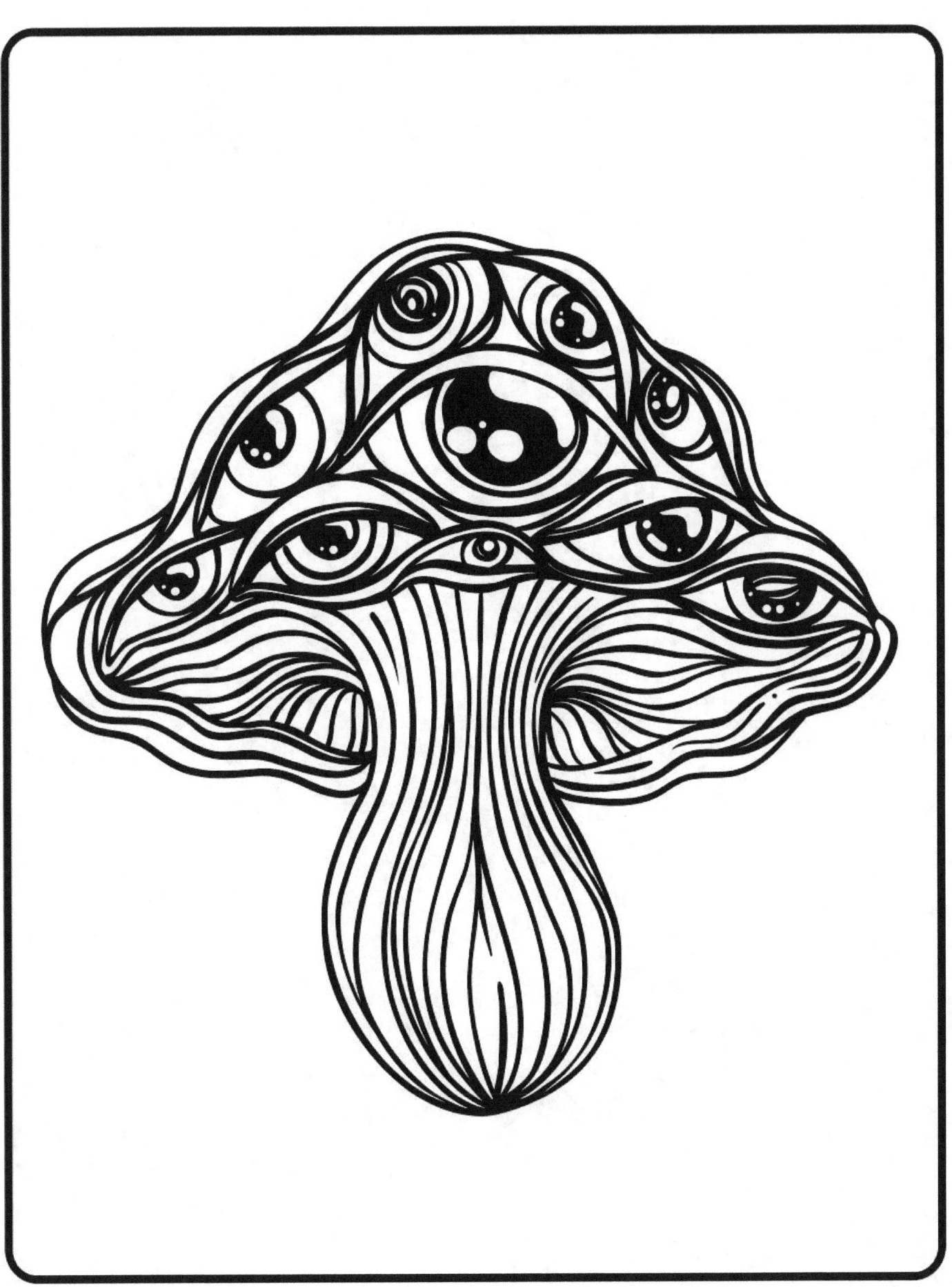

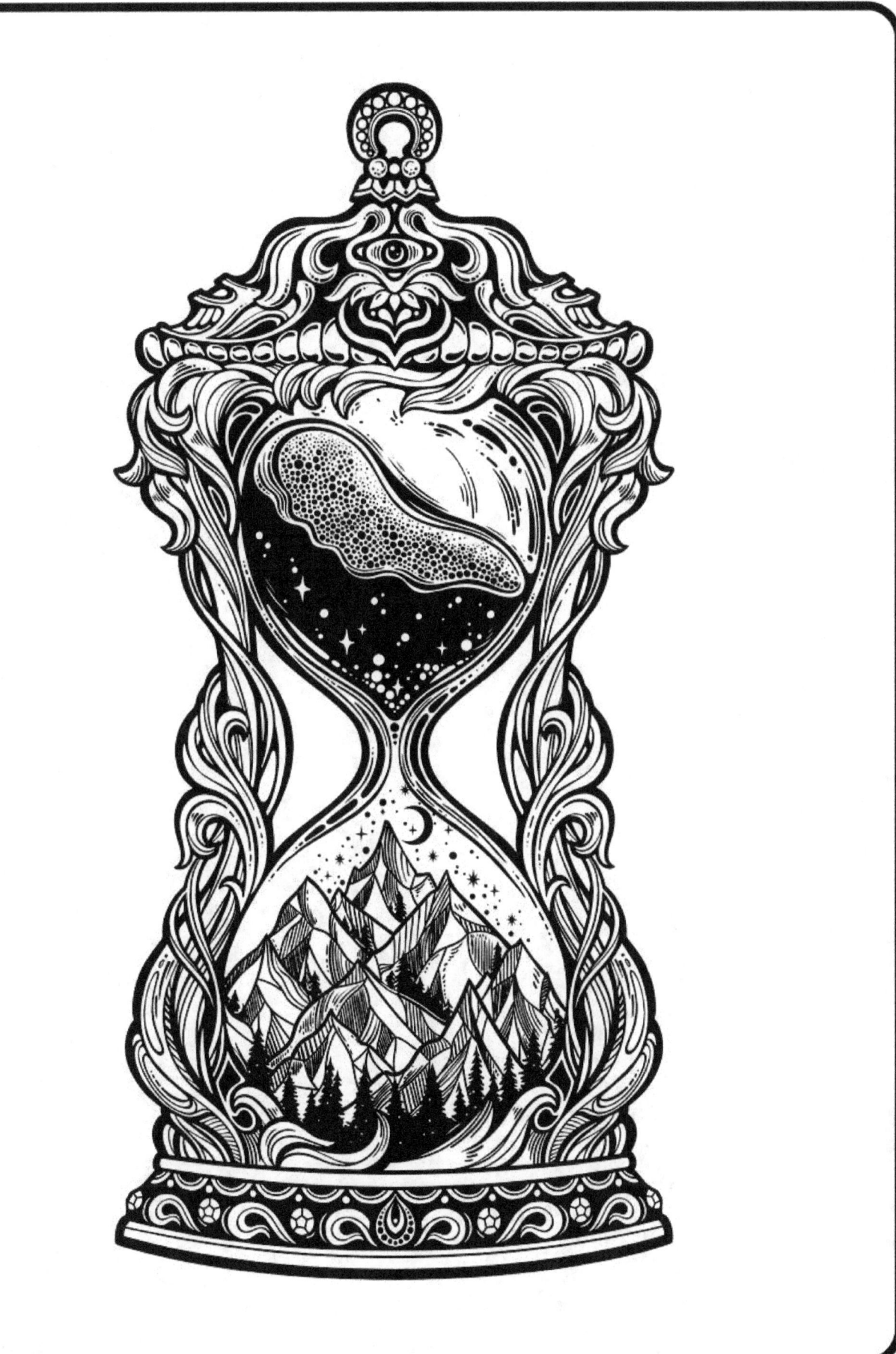

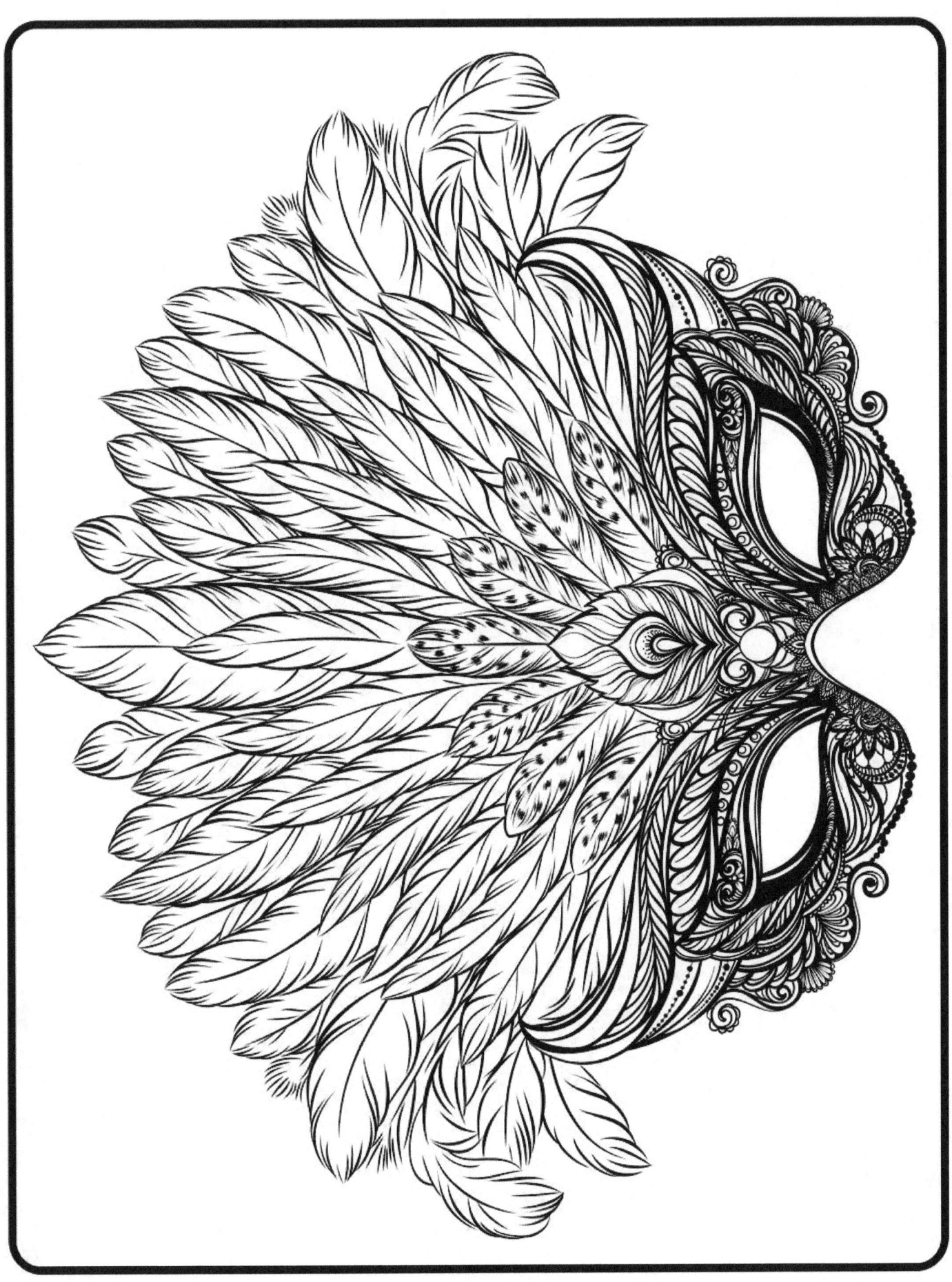

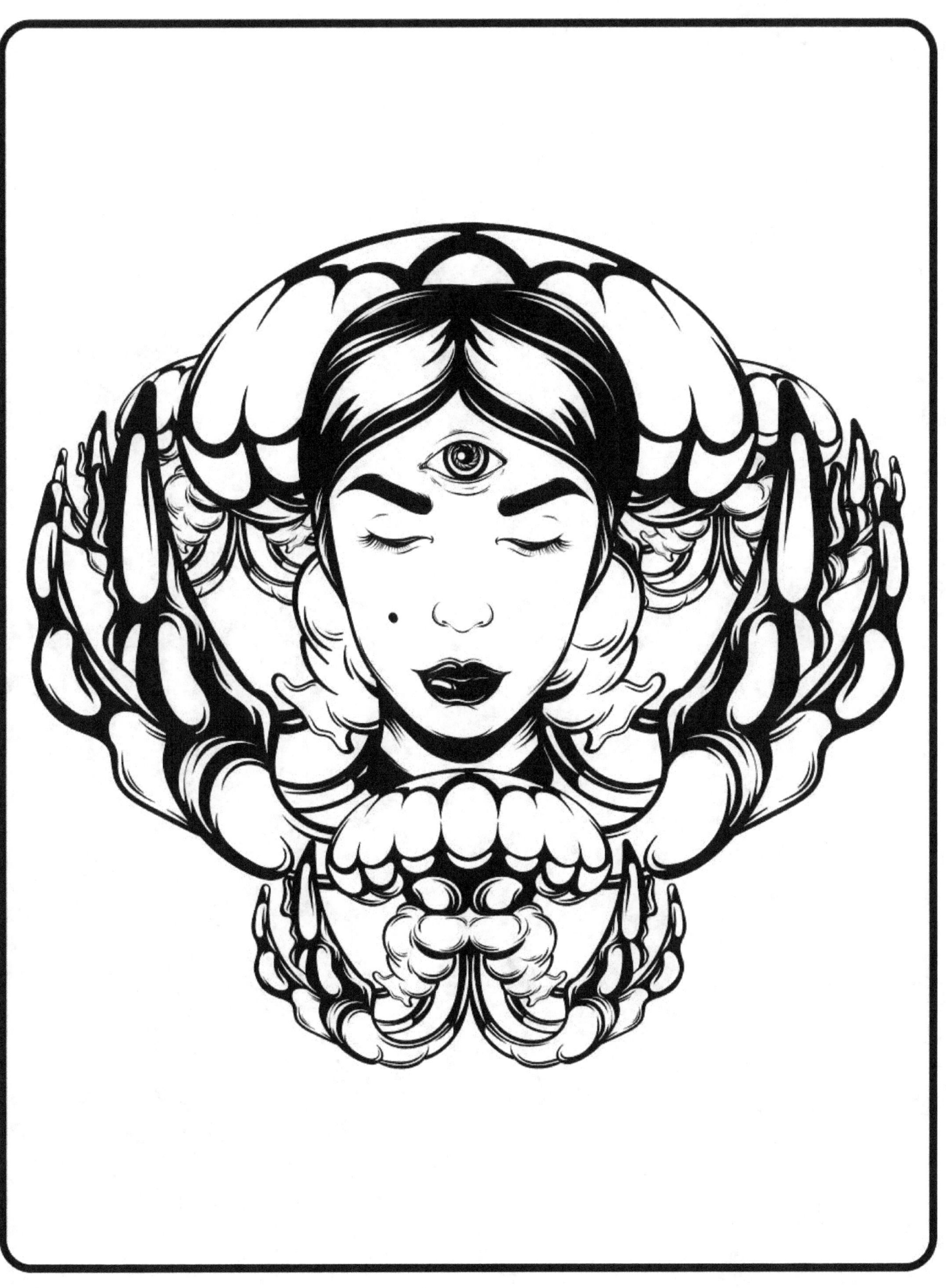

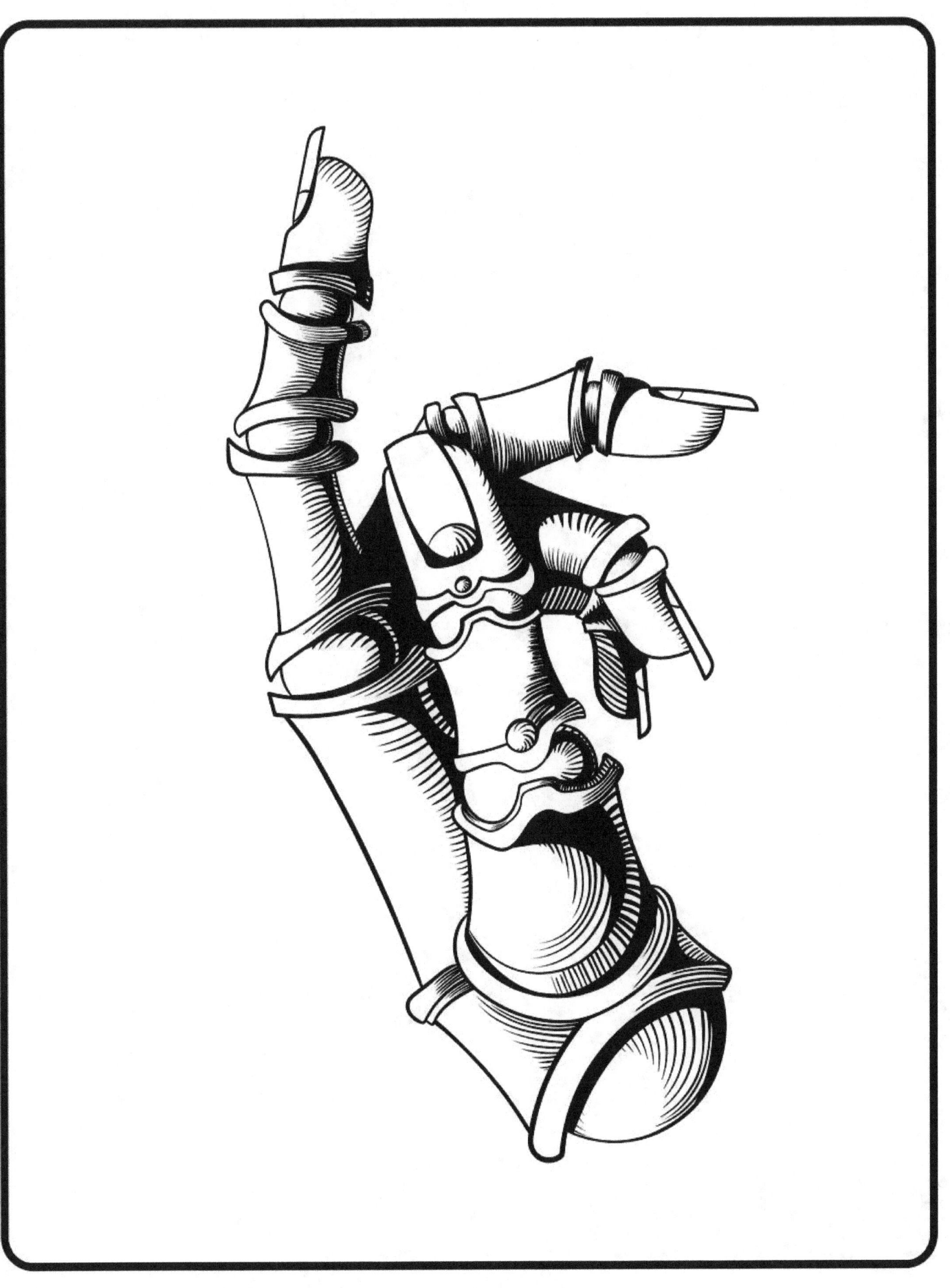

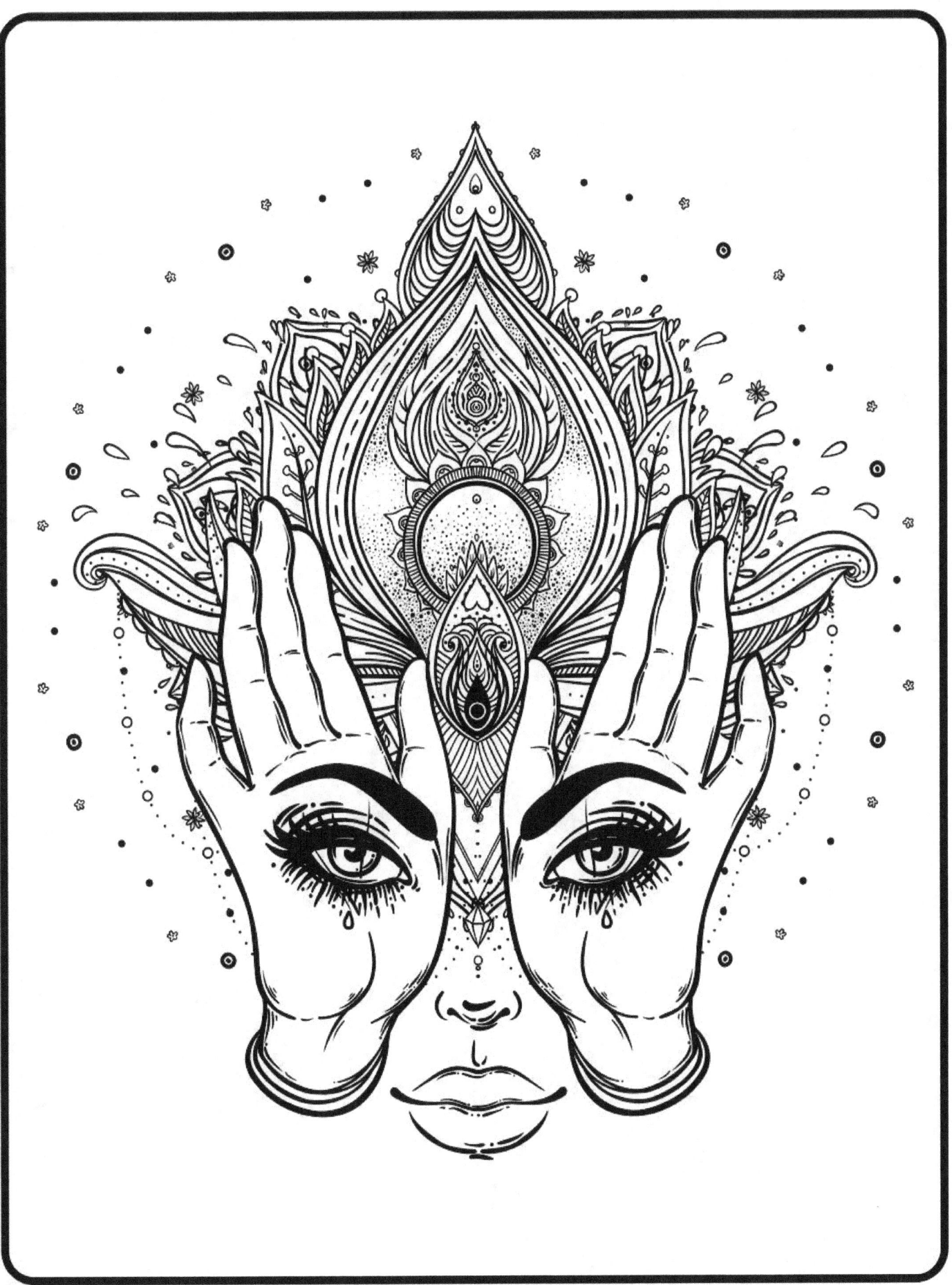

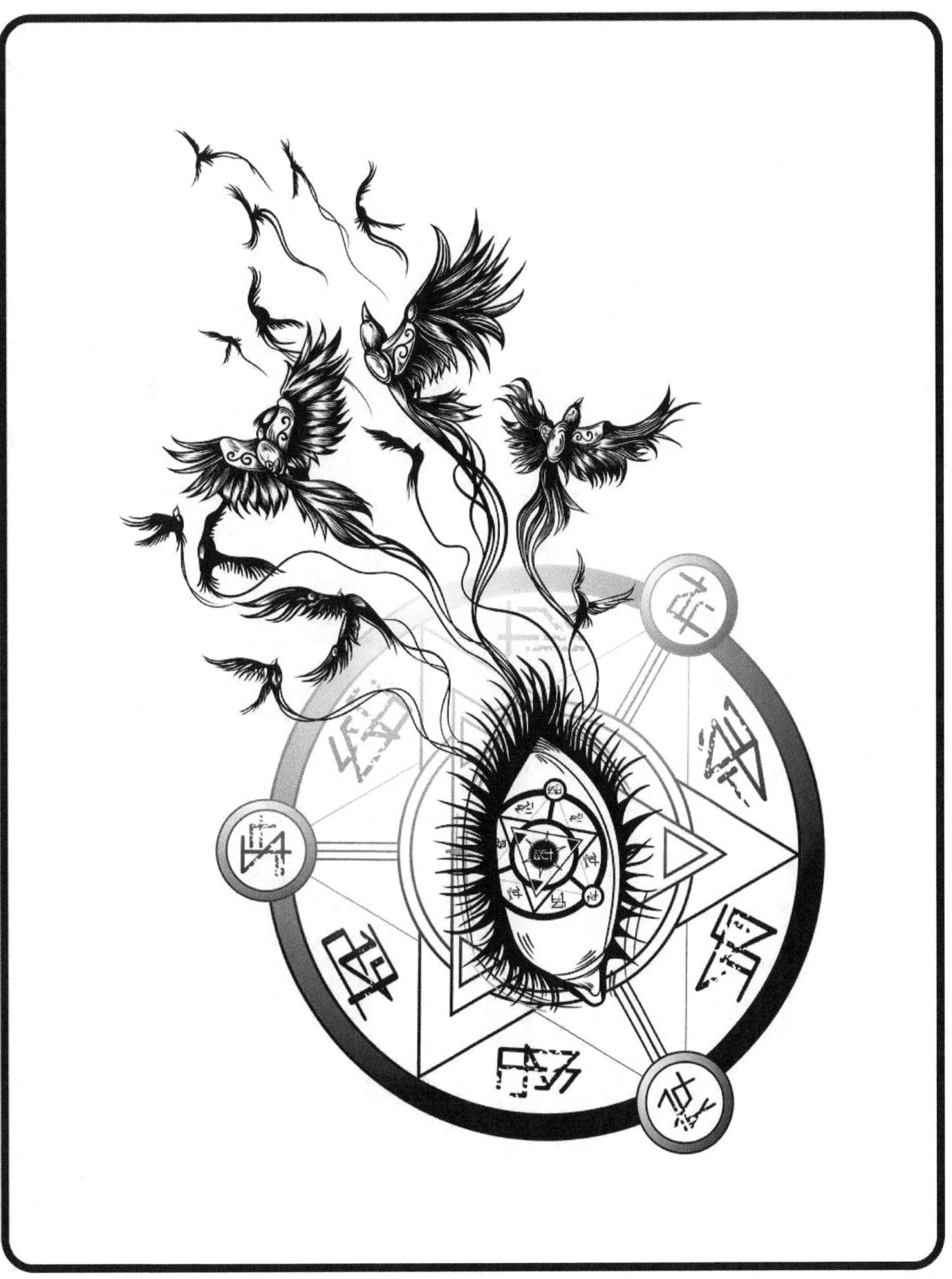

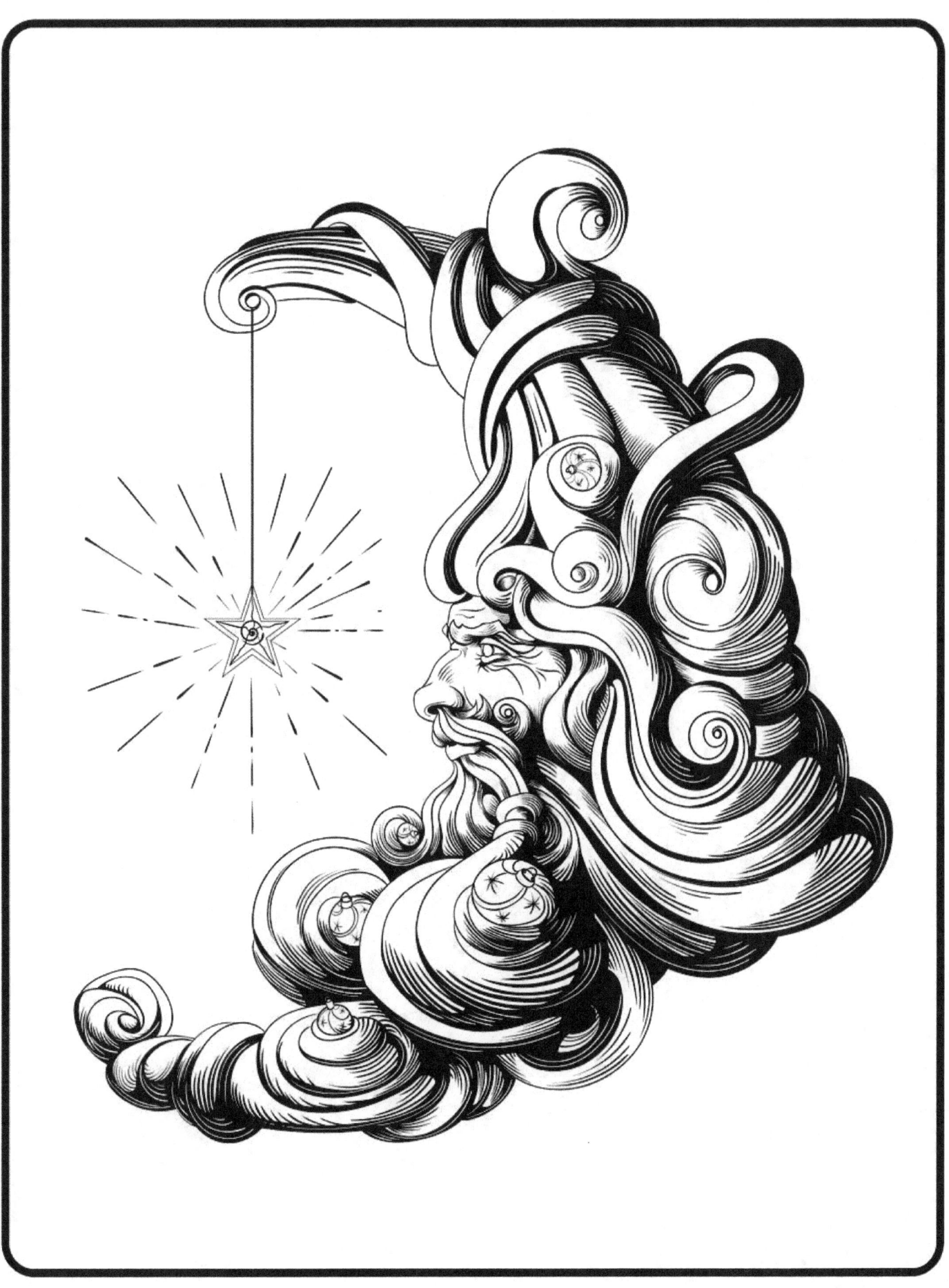

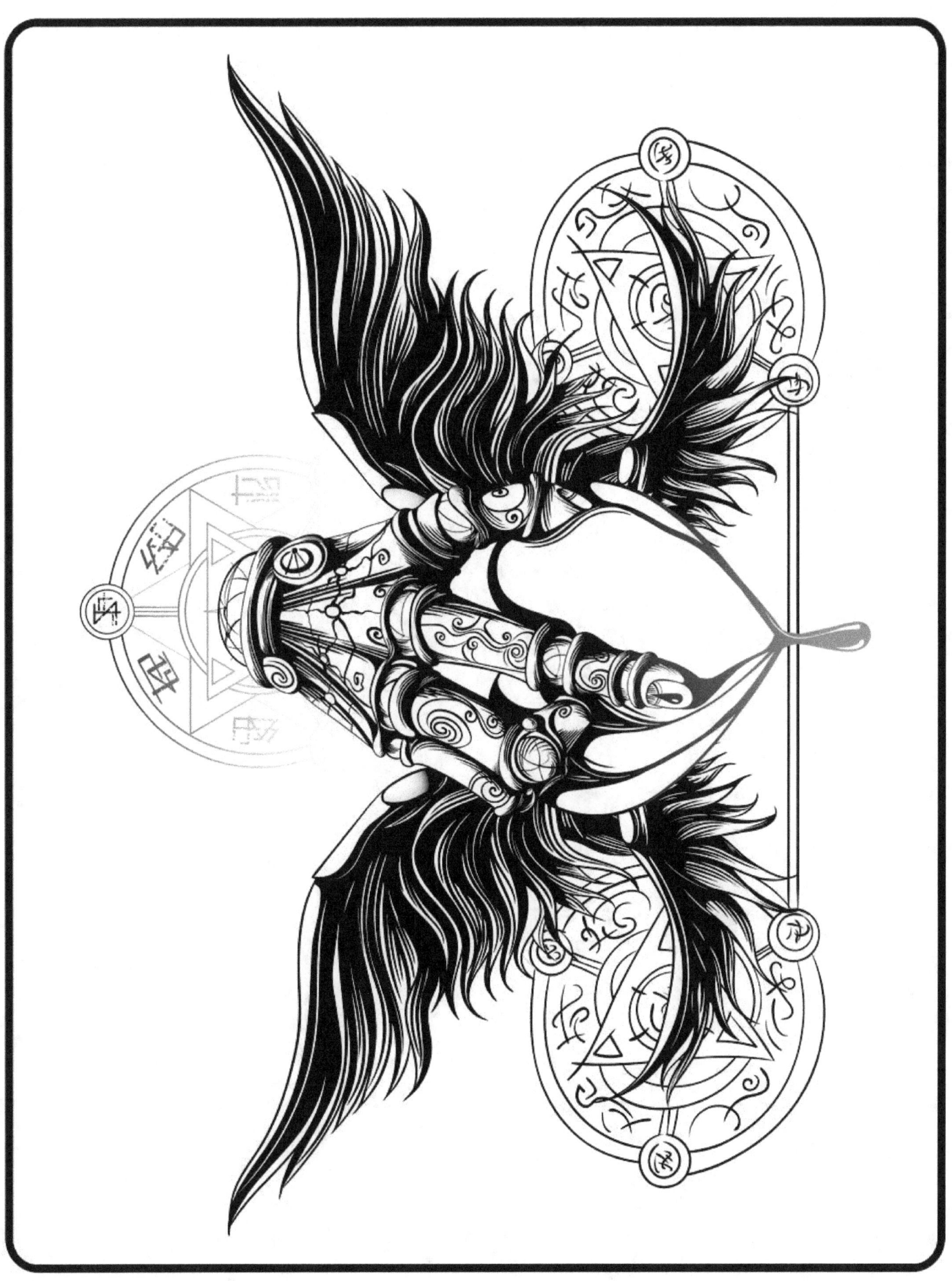

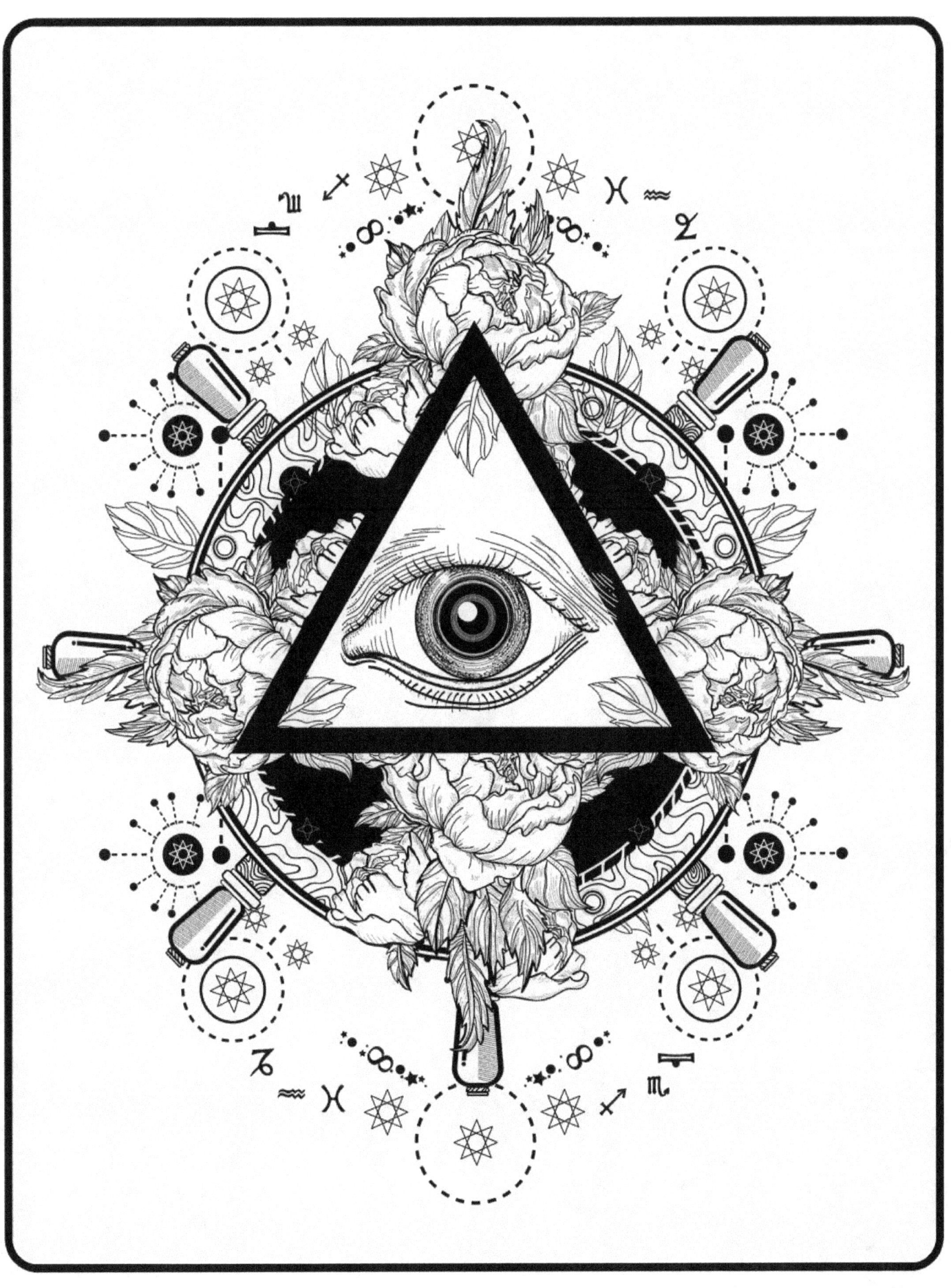

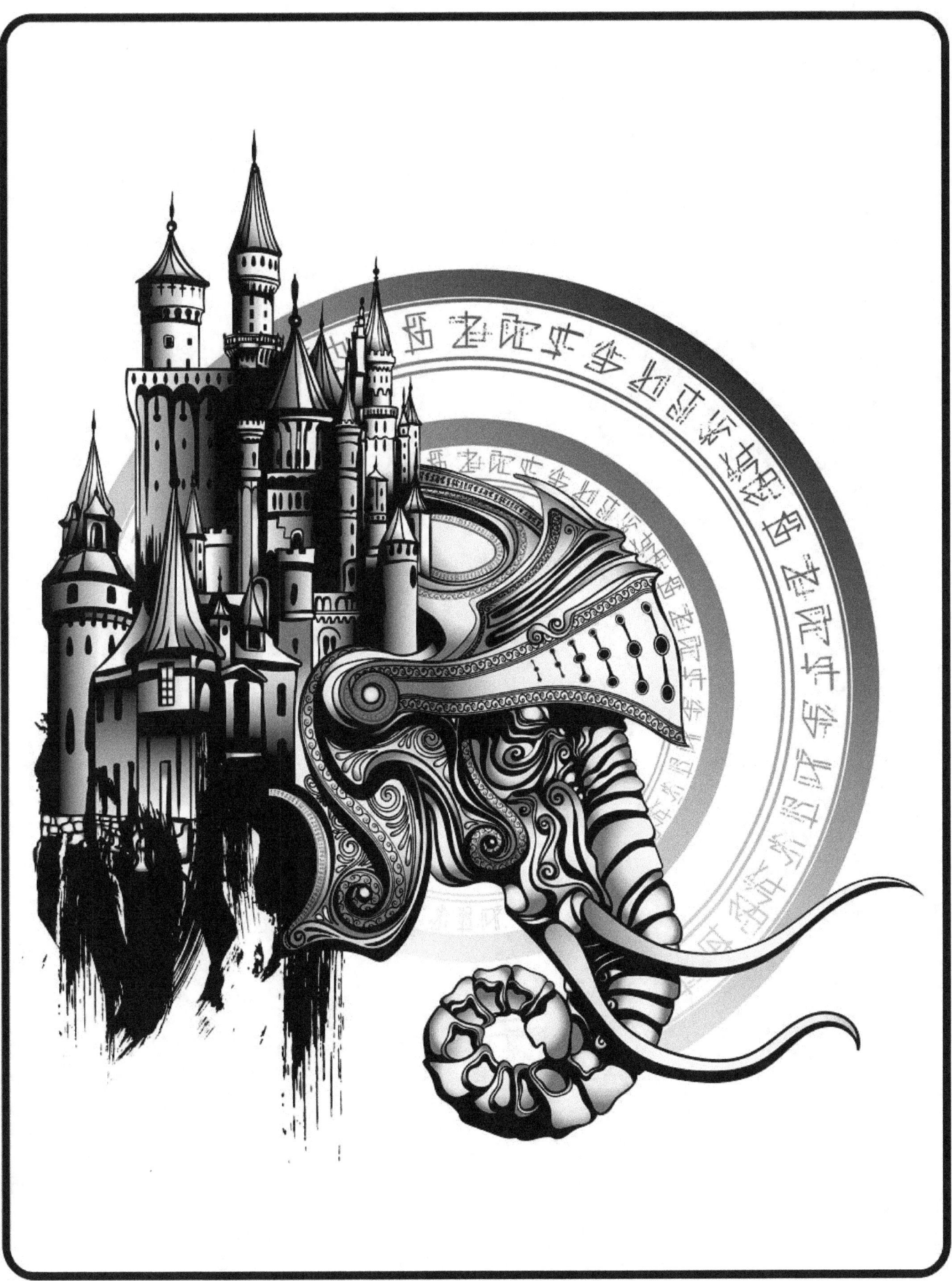

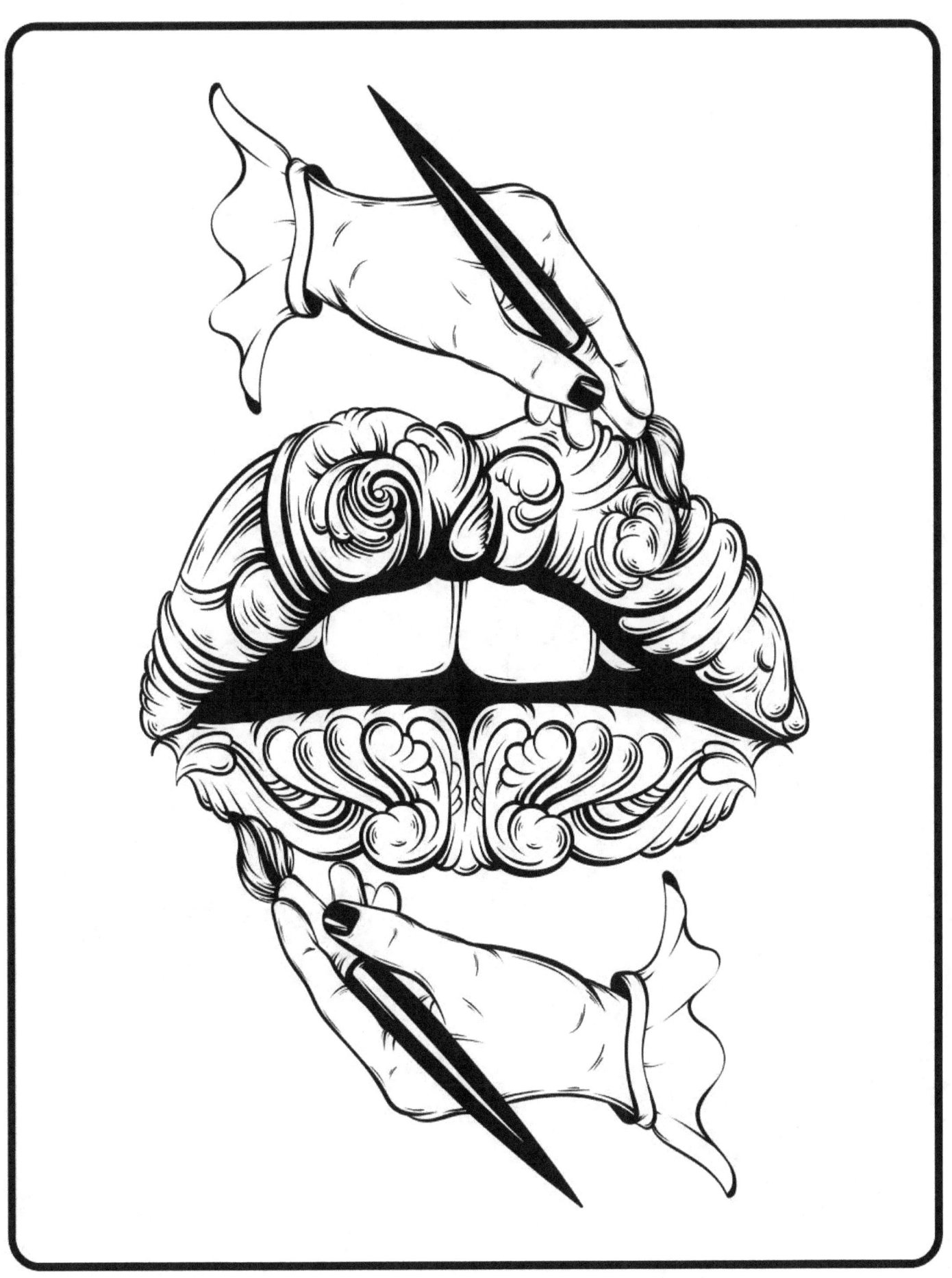

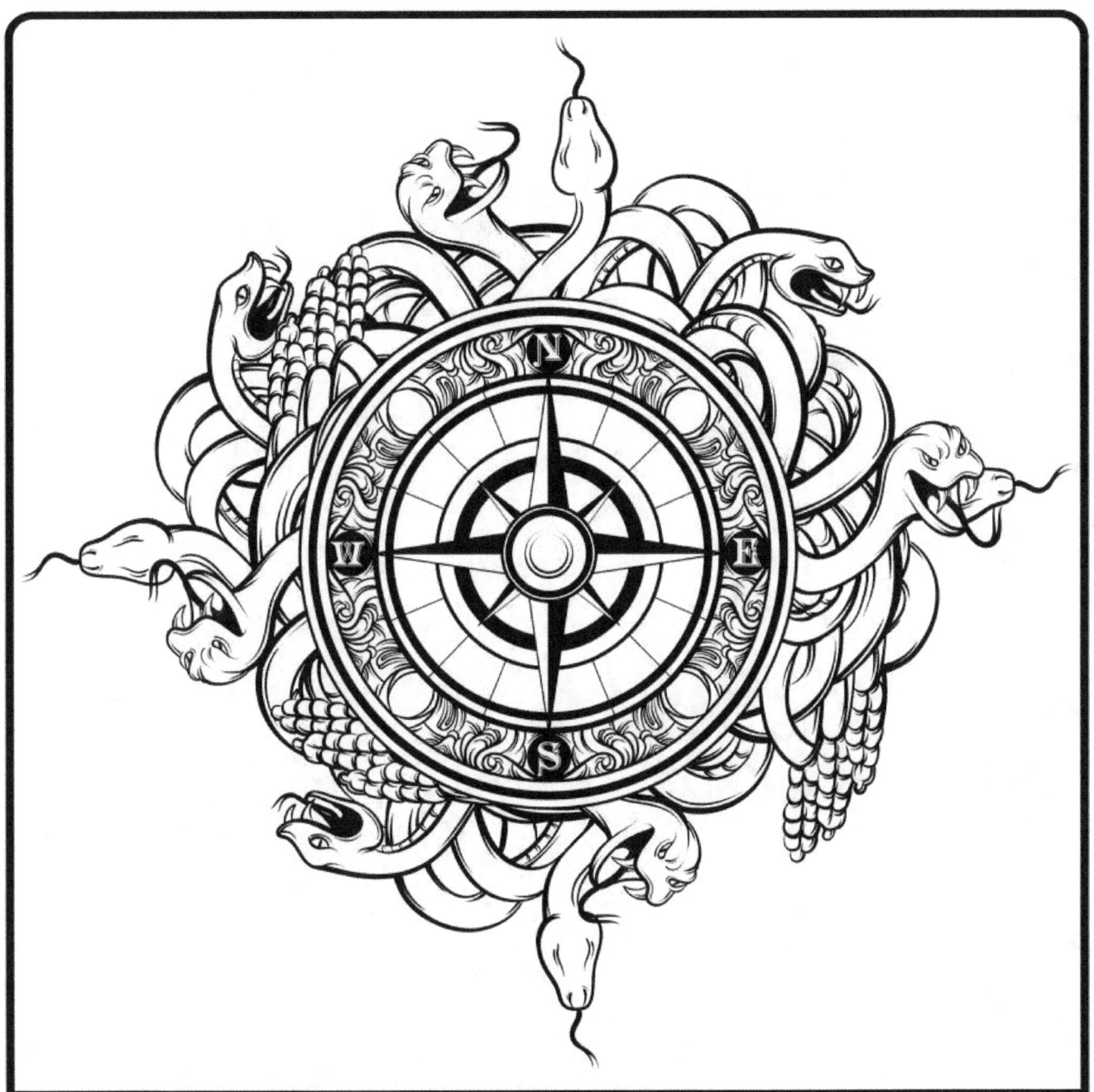

Thank you for buying this book

If you like the book, please consider leaving a review,

it will help author to create better books in the future

www.amazon.com/Katrin-Stark

www.amazon.co.uk/Katrin-Stark